Lost Innocence

A Journey through Abuse and Deception

Tamaramieka Osen

To those who have faced or are currently facing similar experiences with woyinzara, serving as a reminder that you will emerge stronger, and your challenges will eventually subside.

About the Author

The author Osen Tamaramieka Mary Woyinghilayefa is a passionate young girl who discovered her love for storytelling at an early age. Born on October 12th, 2006, she embarked on her writing journey while studying for her A levels. Despite her tender age, Tamaramieka's writing prowess shines through in her debut book, which resonates with readers of all backgrounds.

Tamaramieka's motivation to write this book stems from her desire to create a sense of validation for individuals who have faced similar experiences. Through her heartfelt words, she aims to provide solace and understanding to those who may feel alone or misunderstood. With an emphasis on empathy and connection, Tamaramieka's book serves as a reminder that we are not alone in our struggles.

Despite her youth, Tamaramieka exhibits a maturity beyond her years in her writing style and ability to tackle complex emotions. Her book delves into the depths of the human experience, exploring themes of resilience, growth, and the power of self-acceptance. By sharing someonelse's journey, Tamaramieka invites readers to reflect on their own lives and find inspiration in the face of adversity.

As Tamaramieka continues to develop her writing skills and explore new storytelling avenues, she remains committed to sharing narratives that uplift and empower. With her unique perspective and unwavering determination, she is sure to make a lasting impact on the literary world.

Table of Contents

Chapter 1: The Enigma of Birth

Woyinzara Thompson, a name meaning "God's friend," was born into a world of privilege, surrounded by opulence and extravagance. Her parents, part of the wealthy elite, provided her with every material comfort. Yet, beneath the surface, a mystery shrouded her very existence.

To the outside world, Zara's life appeared idyllic. She lived in a palatial mansion, adorned with luxurious furnishings and exquisite works of art. Her wardrobe boasted designer labels, and her every desire was promptly fulfilled. From extravagant vacations to exclusive events, she was acquainted with a lifestyle that many could only dream of.

But beneath the veneer of privilege and luxury, a deep sense of mystery concealed the true nature of Zara's existence. Her parents, driven by a deep-seated desire to protect her from the harsh realities of her birth, shielded her from the truth. They believed that by surrounding her in wealth, they could safeguard her from the complexities that lay beyond their carefully crafted façade of a perfect life.

Zara's mother, Victoria Thompson, was a formidable presence in her life. A wealthy and controlling woman, Victoria held high expectations for her daughter. She used her powerful influence to shape Zara into a polished reflection of societal norms, adding to the internal conflict that brewed within the young girl. Victoria's expectations and pressure only intensified the sense of disconnection that Zara felt from her true self.

Meanwhile, Zara's father, Richard Thompson, was a man consumed by his own responsibilities and image. As a wealthy and emotionally distant figure, he remained unaware of the abuse his daughter endured. Richard's attention was primarily directed towards preserving the family's status and securing their place within the upper echelons of society. Oblivious to the struggles his daughter faced, he remained emotionally absent in Zara's life.

The dynamics within the Thompson household altered between appearances and the hidden truth. On the surface, their wealth and status created an illusion of perfection, but behind closed doors, Zara struggled with a reality that differed from the perfect image shown to the world.

Yet, as Zara grew older, an inexplicable yearning gnawed at her heart. She sensed a disconnect, an intangible void that defied explanation. Her intuition hinted at hidden truths beyond her conscious understanding. Deep down, she knew that something was missing in her life, but the answers remained elusive, hidden by her parents' well-intentioned deception.

While Zara reveled in the abundance that surrounded her, she couldn't shake the feeling that her identity had been obscured by the trappings of wealth. The material comforts provided no solace for the existential questions that continued to plague her nor did they fulfil the void in her heart. She yearned to find the truth of her origin and discover the essence of her being.

Behind closed doors, Zara immersed herself in books and stories, seeking solace in the tales of individuals who had journeyed through hardship and adversity. These narratives of resilience and self-discovery ignited a spark within her, fueling her quest for truth and meaning. She understood that her path would be one of self-exploration, and she was determined to uncover the enigma that hid beneath the facade.

As Zara delved deeper into her personal journey, she realized that true wealth extended beyond mere material possessions. It resided in the richness of relationships, the authenticity of connections, and the depth of self-understanding. With each passing day, she became more aware of the limitations of her sheltered existence and yearned to break free from the gilded cage that had confined her.

Her childhood seemed like a blurry memory, and there was an unsettling feeling about her seemingly perfect family. Despite being fortunate enough to have a family, Zara couldn't shake the sense of displacement that haunted her. This feeling persisted throughout her life, following her like a looming dark cloud. Zara had spent the enormity of her childhood enduring these thoughts and restlessly dodging questions that seemed to have no answer to them or perhaps, were the wrong questions to ask in such a rational world.

The sense of displacement followed Zara like a haunting shadow throughout her formative years. It was an ever-present companion, a reminder that she was an outsider in her own life. In a world that seemed to prioritize material success and external validation, Zara's thoughts were often met with confusion or dismissal. The wrongness she sensed within the picture-perfect family dynamic felt intangible, difficult to pinpoint or express. Her thoughts were at odds with the rationality of the world, leaving her feeling isolated and misunderstood.

As she grew older, Zara realized that the conventional questions she had been trying to answer were not the ones that truly mattered. It was not a matter of finding the right answers in a rational world but rather asking the right questions that would lead her to the truth.

In the midst of her struggle, Zara experienced a traumatic incident—an attempted rape that shattered her sense of safety and innocence. The scars left behind were not only physical but etched deep within her soul. The traumatic incident pushed her into the depths of despair, leaving her feeling broken and vulnerable.

The details of that fateful day remained vivid in Zara's memory, haunting her every waking moment. As the shadows lengthened and darkness descended, she found herself in a dangerous situation, facing the threat of an attempted rape. The sudden intrusion of violence had shattered the illusion of safety that had surrounded her, tearing apart the innocence she had clung to, fragile and delicate.

In that terrifying moment, time seemed to stand still. Zara's heart pounded in her chest, her breath caught in her throat. The violation she experienced went beyond the physical realm, seeping into the very core of her being. The impact was profound, leaving her feeling violated, broken, and utterly vulnerable.

In the aftermath of the assault, Zara retreated into herself, drowning in a sea of despair and anguish. The shards of her shattered innocence pierced her soul, embedding themselves deeply within her psyche. She dealt with feelings of shame, guilt, and self-blame, questioning her own worth and the nature of the world she inhabited.

As days turned into weeks and weeks into months, Zara's struggle intensified. The trauma she endured acted as a heavy burden that weighed her down, shaping her thoughts, actions, and interactions with others. The once vibrant light within her faded, overshadowed by the darkness that had consumed her.

In her isolation, Zara's shattered spirit yearned for healing, for a way to mend the broken pieces of her soul. Yet, the journey to reclaim her sense of self and find solace seemed insurmountable. The road ahead was filled with darkness, triggering flashbacks and nightmares that reawakened the pain she so desperately wanted to escape.

In her early teenage years, Zara constantly fought with an unexplainable feeling of isolation. She experienced a deep sense of being an outsider within her own world, yearning for a connection she struggled to put into words for others to understand. Despite being surrounded by luxury and excess, she felt like a solitary presence, lost amidst a sea of unfamiliar faces.

At school, she observed her peers forming deep bonds of friendship and camaraderie while she struggled to find her place. She felt isolated despite being surrounded by wealth and luxury. Social interactions baffled her, making her feel like an outsider. She desperately yearned for connection but couldn't fully express her longing.

Unbeknownst to Zara, her mother had battled a debilitating illness, a fact carefully hidden from her. The surrogacy that had brought her into existence was a delicate secret hidden from her throughout her life. Her parents, wanting to protect her from the burden of this truth, shielded her from the knowledge of her unconventional birth.

The absence of this vital information left Zara with a deep sense of confusion and emptiness. She sensed a void within her, an unspoken truth that shaped her perception of the world. This unseen force shaped her perception of the world and fueled her quest for connection and belonging.

Her isolation manifested in various ways. The halls of her extravagant home echoed with the sound of her footsteps as she traversed them alone, her laughter and cries falling on empty walls. The vibrant social gatherings that her parents hosted became mere spectacles, leaving her feeling detached and invisible.

In her solitude, Zara continuously sought solace in the realm of her thoughts and imagination. She delved into books, immersing herself in fictional worlds that provided fleeting moments of companionship and understanding. These literary escapades became a refuge, a sanctuary where she could escape the isolation that plagued her reality.

As the years unfolded, Zara's struggle intensified. She yearned to forge meaningful connections, to be seen and understood by others. But her attempts to bridge the gap between herself and her peers often fell short, leaving her feeling even more isolated and misunderstood. The weight of her secret, unbeknownst to her, had created an invisible barrier between herself and those around her.

She yearned for someone who could see past the facade, someone who would understand the depths of her emotions and embrace her for who she truly was. Little did Zara know that the revelation of her unconventional birth held the key to unlocking the door to her true identity. The knowledge of her mother's illness and the selfless act that had brought her into the world would give her the answers she had been seeking all her early life.

In her search for solace, Zara found herself wandering into the ethereal realm of the supernatural. Ghostly encounters became a peculiar aspect of her life, their presence mirroring her own sense of fragmented existence. These spectral interactions stirred within her a strange mixture of fear and fascination, as if the spirits she encountered were whispering fragments of her own hidden truth.

At times, Zara confided in imaginary friends, vivid characters conjured from the depths of her imagination. These vivid characters became her confidants, offering a sanctuary from the harsh realities she faced. Through these relationships, she discovered the power of imagination and the strength it held in reshaping her reality.

At first, the encounters with the otherworldly filled Zara with a mixture of fear and fascination. Shadows danced across the walls, whispers echoed through empty rooms, and cold gusts of wind brushed against her skin. Yet, there was an undeniable pull that drew her towards these apparitions, an unspoken connection that defied rational explanation. She felt a strange connection with the spirits, as if they held the missing pieces of her own enigmatic puzzle.

In the presence of these apparitions, Zara felt a stirring within her soul—a profound recognition that their whispers and ethereal presence held fragments of her own hidden truth. Their spectral forms became mirrors, reflecting the cracks and crevices of her own existence. While their presence initially evoked fear, she soon realized that they were beckoning her to confront her own ghosts, both literal and metaphorical.

In addition to her spectral encounters, Zara sought solace in the realm of her imagination. In the depths of her mind, she conjured vibrant and captivating characters, her imaginary friends. These imaginary companions became her confidants, providing a sanctuary from the harsh realities of her tangible world. They offered unwavering support, empathy, and understanding—a comfort she struggled to find in the physical realm.

In the face of adversity, Zara discovered her inner strength and resilience. She learned to confront her fears head-on, bravely facing the ghosts of her past and the demons that had haunted her. The mysteries surrounding her birth through surrogacy no longer defined her but instead became a source for her self-discovery and a source of empowerment.

Throughout her journey, Zara's perception of innocence evolved. She recognized that true innocence did not lie in ignorance but in the courage to face the truth and retain one's integrity amidst the darkness. As she shed the layers of deception and abuse, she emerged with a renewed sense of self.

The path to healing proved to be difficult, but Zara discovered that she was not alone. Along her journey, she had found kindred spirits—compassionate souls who offered support, understanding, and a shared journey towards reclaiming lost innocence. They stood by her side, providing a comforting presence and guidance as she navigated the depths of her pain and confusion.

As Zara continued to peel back the layers of her past, she unearthed hidden truths and confronted the shadows that had long haunted her. It was a process that required immense courage and resilience. She faced the darkest corners of her existence, unafraid to delve into the depths of her pain and confront the memories that had shaped her.

Chapter 2: The Surrogacy Secret

Born into a life of privilege, Zara had always known the luxuries that money could bestow. Yet, behind the facade of luxury, she had always sensed an unspoken void, a yearning for a connection that seemed just beyond her reach. Little did she know that her sense of belonging was about to be shattered, leading her on a journey of self-discovery that would test her resilience and redefine her understanding of love, truth, and the essence of family.

As the sun had set on another day in the affluent neighborhood she called home, Zara had found herself on the cusp of an extraordinary revelation. This day was going to change everything in her life as she knew it. An unexpected turn of events propelled her into the heart of her family's history, a history that had been meticulously concealed from her in the shadowy corners of the past.

Pushed under the weight of expectations and the facade of the perfect family, Zara had sought solace in the least likely of places - the attic. The room above, hidden from the glamour of her daily life, harbored dusty boxes containing relics of forgotten times. And within those cardboard containers lay the catalyst for a profound transformation that would challenge the very fabric of Zara's being.

Amidst the chaos and disarray of a world defined by riches, Zara stumbled upon the fragments of a secret long kept from her. The attic became a sanctuary, where she began her quest for the truth - a truth that held the key to unlock the enigma of her existence. Little did she realize that the revelations buried within those old boxes would serve as the catalyst for an emotional journey she never could have imagined.

As Zara delved deeper into her quest for truth, she stumbled upon the long-hidden secret that would forever alter her perception of her identity. It was a scorching summer day when Zara found herself rummaging through old boxes in the attic, seeking solace from the chaos that surrounded her affluent home. Little did she know that within those dusty cardboard containers lay the key to unlock the enigma of her existence.

Tucked away amidst fading photographs and forgotten memorabilia, Zara discovered a weathered journal, adorned with delicate floral patterns. Intrigued, she flipped through the pages, and her eyes widened as she stumbled upon an entry that would change her life forever.

The inked words on the yellowed pages revealed the incredible tale of her birth, shrouded in secrecy and deception. Her heart pounded as she read the story of a courageous woman, her biological mother, who had suffered from a debilitating illness, rendering her unable to conceive. This revelation meant that Zara was not her parents' biological child. She was born through surrogacy.

As Zara stood amidst the boxes in the attic, her hands trembling as she held that weathered journal, a surge of emotions had engulfed her. The weight of the truth bore down on her shoulders like an immeasurable burden, threatening to suffocate her with its gravity. She felt like a ship lost at sea, adrift in a storm of confusion and heartache.

Reflecting on all those years of dissatisfaction and yearning for belonging, Zara's heart ached with a profound sense of loss. She couldn't help but wonder why her parents had chosen to keep the truth hidden from her, denying her the chance to understand her own roots and heritage. The walls she had carefully constructed to protect herself from judgment and vulnerability now crumbled, leaving her feeling exposed and vulnerable.

In the silence of the attic, Zara allowed herself to confront the questions that had haunted her for so long. Did her parents love her any less because she wasn't their biological child? How could she reconcile the love and care she had received all these years with the knowledge that her existence was the result of a surrogate's sacrifice?

She grappled with conflicting emotions - gratitude for the life she had been given and anger at the deception that had shrouded it.

Grief washed over her like a relentless tide, mourning the innocence she had lost and the sense of belonging that had eluded her. The self-assured image she had projected to the world now seemed like a mere facade, a mask she wore to shield herself from the pain of not truly knowing who she was.

In that moment of vulnerability and raw honesty, Zara allowed herself to shed the layers of pretense she had carefully woven around herself. She faced the mirror of her soul, gazing at her reflection with tears streaming down her cheeks. It was not just her physical appearance she saw but the heartache, confusion, and longing that lay beneath the surface.

A whirlwind of emotions engulfed Zara - confusion, disbelief, and a profound sense of loss. The foundation of her identity seemed to crumble beneath her feet. She had always felt a peculiar disconnect with her parents, an unspoken barrier that she could never quite explain. Now, the truth revealed why this emotional chasm existed.

The weight of the surrogacy secret bore down on Zara like an unyielding storm, leaving her emotions in disarray. Night after night, she wrestled with the truth, unable to escape the gnawing questions that plagued her mind. Was she ever truly wanted? Did her parents love her as much as they would a biological child? The constant battle between logic and emotion tore at her heart, leaving it scarred with uncertainty.

Her once blissful home, now seemed cloaked in shadows. Zara watched her parents through a different lens, trying to discern any sign of the secret they had kept so well-hidden. A profound sense of betrayal and abandonment consumed her. If they had lied about something as fundamental as her birth, what else were they hiding?

The mirror became an enemy, reflecting not just her physical appearance but a relentless reminder of her tangled identity. Zara no longer recognized the face staring back at her, as if the very essence of her being had been erased and replaced by a stranger.

In the halls of her prestigious school, she felt like an imposter, wondering if her privileged life was built upon a foundation of deception. She withdrew from her friends, fearing that the truth of her birth would change how they saw her, just as it had changed how she saw herself.

Everywhere she turned, Zara encountered the echoes of her lost innocence, and her world grew smaller as she built walls around her wounded heart. It became easier to hide behind a facade of indifference than to confront the overwhelming emotions that threatened to consume her.

One rainy evening, as thunder rumbled in the distance, Zara sought solace at the old park near her home. The raindrops mingled with her tears as she sat on a lonely bench, staring at the barren tree branches swaying in the wind. Her heart ached for the mother she had never known, and the questions that lay buried within her soul yearned for answers.

Yet, amidst the turmoil, a glimmer of hope emerged. Zara knew that she could no longer hide from the truth, nor could she allow the weight of deception to define her. This newfound knowledge became a beacon of light guiding her towards self-acceptance and healing. The journey ahead was uncertain, but she resolved to embrace it with courage, knowing that confronting the truth was the only way to reclaim her lost innocence and find her place in the world.

In that moment of profound reflection, Zara found strength she didn't know she possessed. As she thought more about the journal, holding onto the truth that had eluded her for so long, a sense of empowerment had stirred within her. She was determined to navigate the stormy waters of her past and uncover the truth that would set her free. With her heart full of hope, Zara took the first step on her transformative journey of self-discovery, knowing that it would lead her to the person she was always meant to be.

The path ahead was not easy; it was filled with obstacles, heartache, and moments of self-doubt. Zara had to confront the powerful elite of her society, who preferred to keep the truth buried in shadows. Yet, with every challenge she faced, her determination only grew stronger.

Through the highs and lows of her journey, Zara had discovered resilience she never knew she possessed. She began to understand that her true worth did not lie in her biological origins but in the strength of her character and her capacity to love unconditionally.

After the fateful discovery in the attic, Zara's behavior had undergone a profound transformation. The weight of the surrogacy secret no longer suffocated her; instead, it acted as a source for change and self-discovery. She found herself oscillating between moments of vulnerability and strength, uncertainty and determination, as she navigated the emotional labyrinth that had become her reality.

At first, Zara withdrew from her family, struggling to come to terms with the revelation and the years of deception that had eroded her sense of trust. Her once warm and vibrant demeanor gave way to guardedness, and she retreated into a cocoon of self-reflection, seeking to make sense of her emotions and find her place in the world.

Yet, as the days turned into weeks and the weeks into months, Zara's behavior gradually shifted. With newfound determination, Zara embarked on a relentless quest for the truth of her surrogacy origins. She reached out to experts in the field, gathering information about the surrogacy process and connecting with others who had been through similar experiences. The search for her biological mother became a driving force, and she longed to understand the woman whose selflessness had brought her into the world.

As she peeled back the layers of deception that had veiled her past, Zara confronted her parents about the surrogacy secret. The conversation was fraught with tension and raw emotions, but it opened the door to healing and understanding. She came to realize that her parents' decision to keep the truth hidden had come from a place of protection, not malice. They had wanted to shield her from the pain of her biological mother's illness and the complexities of surrogacy. In time, this revelation helped bridge the chasm of mistrust, allowing Zara to rebuild her relationship with her parents on a foundation of honesty and empathy.

Zara's journey of self-discovery was far from over, but she faced each challenge with newfound resilience and courage. The emotional turmoil that once consumed her began to transform into a source of strength, molding her into a person of depth and compassion.

With the newfound strength and hope of finding her real mother, Zara started to reframe her perception of identity and belonging. She realized that her worth was not defined by biology or societal expectations but by the love she gave and received, the empathy she showed, and the impact she had on the lives of others.

As Zara stepped into the next chapter of her life, uncertainty still lingered, but she faced it with newfound wisdom and a profound understanding that her identity was a tapestry woven from the threads of her past, present, and the limitless possibilities of her future. Her journey was a testament to the indomitable human spirit, the power of self-discovery, and the enduring hope that lay within each of us.

Her past, once a heavy burden of deception, had become a catalyst for growth and transformation. The revelations about her unconventional birth and the complexities of her family's history had forced her to confront the shadows of her past. In doing so, she had discovered aspects of herself she had never known existed - a depth of resilience, empathy, and strength that had been forged through the crucible of her experiences.

Through her journey, Zara had come to understand that our past does not have to define us, but it undoubtedly shapes us. The trials and tribulations, the hidden secrets, and the unforeseen challenges all contribute to the tapestry of our lives. Like a mosaic, every piece comes together to create a unique and intricate picture of who we are.

Uncertainty, she now realized, was not something to fear, but a canvas for possibility. It was the blank pages of her story that were yet to be written, the twists and turns of fate that could lead to unexpected destinations. Zara had come to embrace the notion that life's greatest gifts often arrived in the form of surprises, unearthing hidden treasures in the depths of our souls.

Chapter 3: The Burden of Expectations

As the sun rose on another ordinary day in Zara's life, a feeling of heaviness settled upon her chest. She lay in her bed, gazing up at the ceiling, lost in her thoughts. The weight of expectations, like a stifling blanket, wrapped around her, suffocating her dreams and desires.

Zara was not your typical teenager. Born into a life of luxury, she was a child of unique circumstances, yet those very circumstances seemed to place an even greater burden on her young shoulders. Raised in opulence, she was surrounded by the finest things money could buy, but all she truly yearned for was a glimpse of authenticity in her world.

Her parents, driven by their own history, had mapped out a predefined route for Zara's future. They envisioned her as a reflection of themselves, a projection of their unfulfilled dreams. But Zara was no mirror; she was a canvas, waiting to be painted with the colors of her own passions and aspirations.

Zara's heart was in a constant battle with her mind. A struggle raged within her—on one side, the desire to please those who loved her, and on the other, an innate need to discover her own path.

Zara's feelings were like two strong forces pulling her in opposite directions. It was as if her heart and her mind were having a big argument. On one side, she really wanted to make her parents happy and proud because she cared about them a lot. But on the other side, there was this deep-down feeling inside her that wanted something different. It was like a voice that said, "Hey, you need to find out what makes you happy and follow that, even if it's not what everyone else wants."

This battle between her heart and mind wasn't easy. It was like a storm inside her, with lightning bolts of doubt and confusion. But in the middle of all that chaos, there was a quiet strength growing in Zara.

It was the realization that she needed to find her own way, even if it meant stepping away from the path her parents had set for her.

And so, Zara's story became a journey of trying to balance these two sides. She wanted to make her parents happy, but she also wanted to be true to herself. It wasn't about ignoring what her parents wished for, but about finding a way to make her own dreams fit into their expectations. It was about finding the courage to say, "I can do things my way and still make you proud."

As the pressure grew, Zara found solace in secret moments. She would escape to the sanctuary of her room, the only place where her thoughts truly belonged to her. Here, she could let her imagination run wild, free from the confines of societal expectations. She would sit by the window, watching the world beyond, yearning to be a part of it on her own terms.

Zara's struggle to reconcile her parents' wishes with her own identity was a journey through a labyrinth of emotions. The weight of their hopes pressed down upon her, and yet, her spirit refused to be crushed. She was determined to navigate the treacherous terrain of self-discovery, to find a way to honor her parents' sacrifices while staying true to the fire that burned within her.

Every day seemed like a tightrope walk for Zara. On one hand, she could hear her parents' voices echoing in her head, filled with their well-intentioned advice and expectations. "Be the best, darling," her mother would say with a warm smile. "We've worked so hard to give you all this, and we want you to have every opportunity." On the other hand, a quiet whisper within her would reply, "But what about what I want?"

Zara's parents, fueled by their own history and experiences, wanted to shield her from hardships they had endured. They believed that the path to success was paved with straight A's, prestigious colleges, and secure careers. They dreamed of her stepping into their shoes, fulfilling their aspirations that they never could.

Yet, Zara was a bird with wings yearning to take flight, not confined to a gilded cage. Deep within her, a fire burned—an unquenchable curiosity and longing for adventure. She would watch the birds soaring in the sky from her window and wonder what it would be like to follow her heart's desires, to explore uncharted territories of her own making.

In the quiet moments of the night, Zara's room transformed into a haven of dreams. With the moonlight casting gentle shadows, she would lose herself in her thoughts. Her diary became a confidante, a space where she could pour out her heart's desires without fear of judgment. There, she penned down her dreams of becoming an artist who captured the world's beauty on canvas, of wandering through quaint alleyways in distant lands, of forging her own identity beyond the confines of societal expectations.

As the days turned into weeks and then months, Zara found herself at a crossroads. The struggle within her intensified, each side pulling her with equal force. She would spend hours staring at her reflection in the mirror, as if hoping to find the answers within her own eyes. "Who am I, really?" she would ask herself, her voice almost a whisper.

It was during a particularly stormy night that Zara had a revelation. The rain tapped on her window like a secret code, and lightning illuminated her room, casting fleeting shadows on her walls. In that moment, it struck her—the battle within her was not a fight to win or lose. It was a journey of integration, of weaving her parents' love and expectations with her own dreams and ambitions.

She realized that her parents' expectations were a testament to their belief in her potential. They saw greatness within her, and though their vision might have been shaped by their own experiences, it was born out of love. Zara understood that she didn't need to reject their hopes; she needed to intertwine them with her own aspirations.

Despite growing up in a fancy house with all the nice things, Zara never felt like a "normal" child. She had seen things and experienced things that other kids her age couldn't understand.

One of Zara's earliest memories was of the time she faced an attempted assault. The incident left scars that weren't just physical; they ran deep within her psyche. As she tried to find her voice again, she realized that the world could be a place of darkness and danger, not just the safe haven her parents wanted her to believe.

To make matters even more complex, Zara had an uncanny ability to see things others couldn't. Ghostly apparitions would occasionally appear to her, sending chills down her spine. She never spoke of these spectral encounters, knowing that her parents would dismiss them as childish imagination or, worse, evidence of something being wrong with her. These experiences further isolated her from her peers, making her feel like an outsider in a world that struggled to make sense to her.

As she grappled with the supernatural, Zara found solace in the companionship of imaginary friends. To her, they were as real as the air she breathed. These invisible confidants were her constant companions, offering comfort and understanding in a world that often felt bewildering. Yet, she knew that sharing this part of her life with anyone else would invite ridicule and scorn.

The classroom was another realm where Zara's struggles played out. While other children seemed to effortlessly form bonds of friendship, she found it difficult to connect. Social interactions felt like intricate puzzles she couldn't quite solve. Her attempts at conversation were often met with puzzled glances or distracted indifference. Zara yearned to belong, to be part of the laughter and camaraderie that seemed to come so naturally to others.

In the midst of all this, her parents' expectations hung over her like a dark cloud. They had big dreams for her, dreams she wasn't sure she could fulfill. Their words, sometimes well-meaning but hurtful, felt like poison seeping into her heart. They would say things like, "You have to be the best," or "You need to live up to our name." These words were like thorns that pricked at her self-esteem, making her doubt her own worth.

Zara realized that these toxic remarks were like roadblocks on her path to healing. Instead of helping her, they were holding her back, making her feel even more trapped. She wanted to heal, to overcome her fears and struggles, but it was hard when those closest to her were unintentionally hurting her with their words.

As Zara confronted the weight of expectations, she realized that she didn't need to be a perfect replica of her parents' wishes. She didn't need to fit the mold of normalcy defined by society. Instead, she learned to find her own identity, embracing the shadows and the light that made her who she was.

Dear reader, Zara's story is a reminder that healing is a process that takes time and effort. It's about embracing our uniqueness, finding the courage to speak up, and seeking the help we need to move forward. Zara's journey shows us that we can turn our struggles into stepping stones toward a brighter future, breaking free from the shackles of expectations to create a life that is truly our own.

As Zara embarked on this journey of self-discovery and empowerment, she knew that being brave was her only option. The path she was choosing was not easy, and she couldn't expect everyone to understand or support her choices. The battle between her own desires and the expectations of her parents was like walking on a tightrope, each step requiring her to find her balance anew.

Despite her parents wanting her to act like other kids, Zara had stayed brave. She faced a heavy feeling in her chest as she thought about the expectations they had for her. She wasn't a regular teenager – her life was unique. But her parents wanted her to be just like them, and this made her feel trapped.

Zara's journey to finding her own identity was not just about defying her parents' expectations. It was also about discovering the power of self-acceptance. As she delved deeper into her interests and passions, she realized that her uniqueness was her strength. She embraced her ability to perceive the world differently, to find beauty in the unconventional, and to connect with people on a deeper level.

One of the most profound lessons Zara learned was that bravery was a daily practice. It wasn't a one-time decision, but a series of small, deliberate steps toward embracing her true self. It meant speaking up when her voice trembled, pursuing her passions even in the face of uncertainty, and being unapologetically herself, no matter the circumstances.

Zara's struggle was like a journey through her emotions. Her parents' dreams were heavy on her, but she didn't give up. She wanted to make them proud, but she also wanted to be herself. She needed to find a way to do both.

While her parents wanted to protect her from difficulties, Zara wanted to be free. She looked at the birds outside her window and wondered what it would be like to follow her own desires.

At night, her room became a place of dreams. With the moonlight, she would write down her dreams in a diary. She wanted to be an artist and explore new places, far from what people expected of her.

As Zara looked back on her journey, she realized something important. When she decided to be true to herself and take a path that wasn't common, it had a big effect on the people around her. She saw that her choices sometimes made others feel uneasy and unsure. They felt this way because her decisions were different from what they were used to.

Zara saw that as she got stronger in standing up for what she believed in, some people didn't feel comfortable. Her choice to do things her own way made them think about their own wishes and dreams that they hadn't explored. It was like her journey made them see their own worries and fears.

Through these experiences, Zara understood that her personal growth also impacted others. Some people didn't like her doing things differently, but others felt motivated to be themselves too. She handled these situations by being patient, understanding, and knowing how people think and feel.

Zara's story taught an important lesson: when you choose to be different, it can make people think about themselves. It's not because being different is bad, but because it makes them reflect on their own lives. Her story showed that welcoming all kinds of people and celebrating everyone's uniqueness makes the world more interesting. It encourages people to find out who they really are and be okay with it.

Chapter 4: Sent to a Rural Host Family

Life has a funny way of leading us down unexpected paths. Just when you think you have a grasp on things, a twist comes along that shatters your reality and forces you to navigate uncharted waters. Zara's journey was no different, as she found herself on a new adventure that would forever change her perspective on life.

The decision to send Zara to live with a host family in a rural area was made with good intentions, or so her parents believed. They thought it would be an opportunity for her to experience a different way of life, to be disconnected from the world of privilege she had grown accustomed to. But what they didn't fully comprehend was that this change would be a pivotal chapter in Zara's journey, one that would challenge her in ways she had never imagined.

Life was taking Zara on a new adventure. Instead of staying home, she was sent to live with a different family in the countryside. This choice had its ups and downs, and it's important to see how it all unfolded.

Zara struggled at first. No Wi-Fi, no comfy room, just the bare basics. But as time passed, she started seeing things differently. The absence of all the city buzz gave her space to think, to discover things she never knew about herself.

Out in the fields, watching the stars, Zara realized she could paint. Yeah, she had this artistic thing hidden beneath all that city noise. And you know what else? Those weird ghostly things that would sometimes show up? They didn't go away. She was still seeing them, but not as much. It was like her new surroundings had their own way of dealing with it.

Leaving behind the towering skyscrapers and bustling streets, she found herself amidst rolling hills, open skies, and the soothing embrace of nature. The air seemed crisper, the stars brighter, as if the universe itself was trying to tell her something. This shift was not just a change in scenery; it was a step towards self-discovery, an opportunity to step out of the shadows cast by others' expectations.

In this new world, there were good moments and challenges. On one side, she got to run around in open fields and enjoy nature's simple beauty. Kids her age became her new friends, and they didn't know her past. It felt like a fresh start, a chance to just be herself without any worries.

But of course, new things can be a bit tricky too. Adjusting to a different way of life, with new people and their own rules, wasn't always easy. The people and their habits were like pieces of a puzzle she was trying to solve. Yet, in these challenges, there were opportunities to learn, grow, and become stronger.

Did everything go smoothly? Not exactly. Life in the countryside brought its own set of challenges. Merging her old life with this new one sometimes felt like fitting two puzzle pieces that didn't quite match.

So, was everything perfect? No, because life isn't just about black and white. It's a mix of colors and shades, and that's what makes it interesting.

Living with the host family proved to be an eye-opening experience. Their way of life was simple, rooted in hard work and connection with nature. The family members greeted each day with a sense of purpose, tending to their land, animals, and each other with unwavering dedication.

While she was navigating this new chapter, Zara remembered the tough times she'd been through. The time when something scary almost happened to her. Those memories were like scars, but they also showed her how strong she could be. They proved that she had the power to overcome difficult situations.

Even the things that made her feel different, like seeing strange things and having imaginary friends, became something special. They revealed that being unique was a strength. It was like having a secret power that only she possessed.

And her parents? They wished the best for her, even if they didn't always understand everything. They hoped she'd be like them in certain ways. Yet, her time with the host family taught her that she could be herself and still make her parents proud. It was about weaving her dreams together with theirs.

So, her experience with the host family didn’t solve all her problems completely. But it did show her that life is a journey, not just a destination. It's about growing, learning, and adapting along the way. The events of the past were like pieces of a puzzle that were still coming together to form a bigger picture.

But it wasn't all sunshine and rainbows. Zara had her past haunting her – memories of something terrible that happened to her. And this new family, they had their own troubles too. They seemed all happy and together on the outside, but behind closed doors, there was a lot they were hiding.

Zara learned a big lesson here – things aren't always what they seem. People have their own struggles, their own secrets. And that's okay. It's a reminder that we're all human, dealing with our stuff.

As the days turned into months, Zara changed. She was still Zara, but a stronger version. She faced her fears, embraced her talents, and saw through the facades people put up. This whole experience, the good and the not-so-good, molded her into someone who could handle life's darkness.

Zara's past wasn't just a tiny rain cloud in her life; it was more like a storm that had been following her around. Those memories of that awful thing that happened to her, they were like shadows that just wouldn't go away. They whispered doubt and fear in her ear, making her question everything, including herself.

And this new place, well, it was unsettling for her. It was like stepping into the unknown, and the unknown had never been her friend. The open spaces, the quiet nights – they were like a canvas for her mind to paint all those dark memories on. The scars she carried inside her didn't disappear just because the scenery changed.

But amidst all this, Zara was learning a lesson that hit her like a lightning bolt – life's not a simple puzzle. People's lives are messy, and everyone's got their own struggles. That family she was living with? They looked like they had it all together, but behind those closed doors, there were things they were dealing with. It was a big wake-up call that appearances can be deceiving, and it's okay to not have it all figured out.

As the calendar pages turned and the months rolled on, Zara was transforming. She was still Zara, but now she was a Zara who could face her fears head-on. She started owning her talents, like that artistic side she never knew she had. And those facades people wore? She saw right through them. She had become a version of herself that was tougher, wiser, and ready to tackle whatever life threw her way.

Here's the bottom line: life is a mix of bright days and stormy nights. Zara's journey was a testament to that. She taught herself that even when the past won't let go and new places are scary, there's a fighter inside us that can rise up. Tough experiences don't break us – they mold us into someone who's stronger, more compassionate, and deal with the hardest moments of our life.

Zara's journey was far from ordinary. She had a knack for seeing things that others couldn't. Ghostly apparitions, imaginary friends – her world was a blend of reality and the unknown. But her parents had no clue. They were too caught up in their own world of material possessions to realize the depth of her feelings.

Imagine growing up with a secret world, where shadows held secrets and imaginary friends were as real as the air you breathe. Zara's life was anything but typical. And her parents thought they were doing right by giving her all the luxuries money could buy. Little did they know, all she truly yearned for was a glimpse of authenticity in her world.

You see, her parents believed that success was measured by the things you own. Their love was real, but their understanding was clouded by their own aspirations. They wanted Zara to be a reflection of their dreams, but all she wanted was to be herself.

Through every struggle, every twist and turn, Zara held on to her individuality. She proved that life isn't about fitting into a mold, it's about embracing your uniqueness and making your own path. Her journey was a lesson that healing takes time, and finding your identity is a courageous act.

So, as Zara's rural adventure continued, she carried her past, her struggles, and her newfound strength with her. She was like a puzzle that was finally coming together, piece by piece. And that's the beautiful thing about life – it's a journey of self-discovery, of uncovering the layers that make you who you are.

Zara's story isn't just about one girl's journey; it's a reflection of the battles many of us face. It's about breaking free from the shackles of expectations, about embracing our uniqueness and using our struggles as stepping stones towards a brighter future.

Life had never been ordinary for Zara, and that's what made her shine. Her ability to see beyond the surface, to find strength in adversity, is a testament to the power within all of us. It's a reminder that even when life feels like a storm, we can find our way through the darkness and into the light.

Her parents' intentions were pure, but their understanding was limited. They thought material possessions were the answer, but Zara showed them that the real treasure lies within – the courage to be yourself, unapologetically.

So, dear reader, as you close this chapter of Zara's journey, remember that healing is possible, dreams are worth chasing, and the road to self-discovery is a path well worth taking. Zara's story is a beacon of hope, a reminder that even in the face of adversity, we can rise, transform, and create a life that's uniquely our own.

Chapter 5: Shadows of Abuse

As Zara continued to navigate her new life in the countryside, a longing to understand her own origins grew stronger. She had always felt different, but the pieces of her puzzle didn't quite fit together. Questions swirled in her mind like leaves caught in a gust of wind. Who was she? Where did she truly come from? And why did she feel this unexplainable connection to the unknown? Little did she know, the answers she sought were buried beneath layers of deception and buried truths.

Life is a complex tapestry of experiences, some beautiful and uplifting, others harsh and unforgiving. Just as Zara began to find her footing in her new rural environment, a sinister darkness crept in, shattering her sense of security and unraveling the fabric of her reality.

Within the seemingly calm walls of the host family's home, a storm raged in silence. The very people who were supposed to provide shelter became the source of Zara's torment. It's a harsh truth, but abuse can find its way into the most unexpected corners of our lives.

The shadows grew longer as Zara's harrowing encounters with abuse emerged. The physical and emotional wounds inflicted upon her were scars that ran deeper than the eye could see. Her spirit, once vibrant and full of hope, was now shrouded in fear and confusion.

The abuse was like a storm that would not pass. It thrived in secrecy, lurking behind smiles, only revealing its true face when no one else was around. Zara's heart, already burdened with her own struggles, now carried the weight of this darkness.

The assaults, both physical and emotional, were a brutal reminder that the world could be a place of unimaginable pain. The scars left behind were not just on her body; they scarred her soul. The sanctuary she had sought in the countryside turned into a prison, and the faces that should have been sources of comfort became her tormentors.

Living in constant fear became Zara's new reality. The walls closed in, and the world outside felt like a distant dream. The once open skies and rolling hills seemed to mock her, as if they were oblivious to her suffering. It's a terrifying place to be, trapped in a cycle of pain with seemingly no way out.

As Zara's journey continued, she found herself grappling not only with her past struggles but with the present nightmare she was living. It was a journey through a heart-wrenching struggle of emotions, where darkness threatened to consume her. But here's the thing about darkness – it can never truly dim the light within us.

Despite the unbearable weight of the abuse, Zara's spirit held on. It's a testament to the human capacity for resilience and the unbreakable will to survive. She clung to the fragments of her identity that the abuse couldn't take away, seeking solace in the memories of her dreams and the strength of her own heart.

In the midst of the shadows, Zara's story stands as a beacon of hope. It's a reminder that even in the darkest of times, there is a spark within us that can ignite a fire of change. It's a call to action for us all – to recognize the signs of abuse, to lend a helping hand to those who need it, and to create a world where no one has to suffer in silence.

Zara's world had turned into a relentless storm, with the abuse as its raging core. Each day blurred into the next, a terrifying loop of fear and pain. The scars on her body were matched by the scars on her heart – wounds that cut deep into her sense of self-worth. It wasn't just the physical harm that hurt; it was the shattering of her innocence.

The abuse had awakened the demons of her already darkened past. The memories she had fought so hard to suppress resurfaced with a vengeance, combined with the new horrors she faced. It was like her past was a haunting ghost that had finally found its voice, whispering its cruel messages into her ear.

Those strange encounters she had tried to forget, the time she was almost assaulted, the isolation she felt as she grappled with her unique abilities – they all collided in a perfect storm of pain. It was as if the universe had conspired to break her, to strip away the last of her innocence.

Zara's parents, oblivious to the true depth of her suffering, continued to believe that material possessions and a life of privilege would shield her from life's harsh realities. They never realized that beneath the facade of luxury, their daughter was drowning in a sea of agony. It's a painful truth that sometimes those who are closest to us can also be the most blind to our pain.

But here's the incredible thing about human resilience – even in the face of the darkest nights, the human spirit can find a way to survive. Despite the abuse that sought to crush her, Zara's strength flickered like a stubborn flame. She yearned for a way out, a chance to reclaim the life that had been stolen from her.

As the days turned into weeks and then months, Zara's determination grew. She knew that she couldn't let the abuse define her, that she had to find a way to break free from its suffocating grip. It was a battle, a war within herself, fought in the shadows where no one else could see.

The turning point came when Zara realized that she wasn't alone in her struggle. The pain she carried, the wounds she bore, were not hers to bear alone. It was a revelation that sometimes, the greatest strength can be found in seeking help. With newfound courage, she confided in someone she could trust – a friend, a mentor, who extended a lifeline when she needed it most.

Reaching out for help was like opening a door to a world she thought had been locked away. It was a step towards healing, towards reclaiming her shattered identity. It wasn't an instant fix; it was a process, a journey that required immense courage. But with each step, Zara was piecing herself back together.

The impact of abuse on Zara's life was profound, but it was not the end of her story. It was a chapter, a painful detour that tested her resilience and ignited her inner strength. Her journey through abuse and deception was a crucible, forging a version of herself that was unbreakable, a spirit that could rise from the ashes.

The scenes of being molested by her host father were etched into Zara's mind like a horrifying nightmare – a chilling collection of moments that replayed in the darkness of her thoughts. The man who was meant to be her guardian had become a tormentor, a monster in the guise of a father figure. Each encounter was a nightmare she couldn't escape.

She vividly remembered the first time it happened. The weight of his presence, his drunken breath, the malicious glint in his eyes – they all made the house a storm of terror. The room that once felt like her safe place became a prison of fear, each corner haunted by his scary figure.

The abuse was not just physical; it seeped into every fiber of her being. It was the way his words sliced through her like daggers, leaving wounds that no bandage could heal. The insults, the threats, the manipulation – they were all part of the twisted mind the host father had.

The impact on Zara was devastating. Her sense of self crumbled, replaced by a suffocating self-loathing. She questioned her worth, internalizing the belief that she deserved the pain inflicted upon her. The world outside seemed to blur into a haze, disconnected from the nightmare she was living.

The abuse impacted her every thought, her every move. She walked on eggshells, afraid to provoke his wrath, tiptoeing through life. The vibrant girl she used to be hid in the shadows, replaced by a shell of a person who just wanted to survive.

Each time he lashed out, a piece of her soul shattered. The bruises on her body were painful reminders of her vulnerability, but it was the scars on her heart that cut the deepest. She was trapped in a cycle of torment, caught between the fear of the present and the haunting memories of her past.

The impact on her relationships was very deep. The difficulty she had in making friends before was magnified now. Trust had become the hardest thing to do. The world outside felt hostile, a place where danger lurked behind every smile. There were monsters hiding in plain sight, and the thought of being attacked by one haunted her mind day and night.

The darkness within her became a constant companion, whispering doubts and fears into her ear. The ghosts she had encountered as a child were no longer confined to her imagination; they were reflections of the torment she endured. Even her imaginary friends seemed distant, unable to shield her from the harsh reality she faced.

But amidst the pain, a glimmer of resilience remained. Zara's spirit was not completely burned out; the flame within her rose like a candle in the wind. The same determination that had carried her through her previous struggles now served as a beacon of hope. She clung to the belief that there had to be a way out, a path to liberation from the prison she was trapped in.

As the weight of the abuse grew heavier, Zara's need for escape intensified. She yearned for freedom, for a life where the shadows of abuse didn't cast their long reach. The decision to break her silence was not easy, but it was an important turning point. With courage, she yearned to confide in a person she could trust, revealing the horrors she had endured.

This act of vulnerability would be a declaration of war against the darkness that had enveloped her. It was a cry for help, a plea to be seen and heard. And as the truth would come to light, she could feel the warmth of empathy, the reassurance that she was not alone. The road to healing was still long and difficult, but for the first time, Zara felt all alone in her misery.

The impact of the abuse on Zara was deep and lasting. It left scars that went beyond the physical, marking her soul with a pain that seemed insurmountable. But her journey was far from over. The wounds she carried would eventually become the battle scars of a survivor, a testament to her strength and resilience.

As you continue to read about Zara's journey through abuse and deception, remember that her story is not just about the pain she endured; it's about her unwavering spirit to reclaim her life. It's a reminder that even in the darkest corners of existence, the human heart has the capacity to heal, to find light, and to rise above the shadows.

For children like Zara, who have faced the horrors of abuse, the wounds often run deep and silent. The trauma they endure can alter the way they view themselves and the world around them. Their innocence, once a beacon of purity, becomes tainted by fear and mistrust.

The scars of their past experiences can manifest in various ways – from difficulty in forming healthy relationships to struggles with self-esteem and self-worth. The road to healing is often filled with challenges and setbacks. Yet, it's a journey that speaks to the indomitable spirit within each survivor. With time, support, and self-discovery, they can gradually mend the shattered pieces of their psyche.

As you turn the pages of Zara's journey through abuse and deception, remember that her story is not just one of pain; it's a story of transformation. It's a tale of how the human spirit can rise from the ashes, how wounds can heal, and how the power of truth and resilience can pave the way for a brighter future. And as you read on, you'll witness Zara's journey of breaking free from the chains of abuse, unveiling the strength she never knew she had, and finding her way back to the light.

As you continue to read about Zara's journey, remember that her story is not just about the darkness; it's about the light that shines through even the deepest cracks. It's about the power of hope, the strength of community, and the human capacity to triumph over adversity. Zara's journey serves as a reminder that even in our darkest moments, we have the power to reclaim our lost innocence.

Chapter 6: The Isolated Journey

Life can be like a whirlwind, spinning you in unexpected directions. For Zara, the aftermath of the assault was like stepping into a new reality, one filled with pain and isolation. It was as if the ground beneath her had given way, and she was free-falling into an abyss of confusion and despair.

The incident left Zara deeply scarred, both physically and emotionally and mentally. The shadows of that traumatic event clung to her like a relentless storm cloud. She found herself in a constant battle, trying to make sense of the senseless, to heal wounds that ran deeper than the surface. It was a solitary journey, one that she had to undertake with unwavering determination.

The first school after the incident was a daunting place. Every corner seemed to hide potential threats, every face a potential reminder of her darkest hour. Zara felt like a lonely traveler navigating a dangerous path, always on guard, always wary. The once bustling hallways now felt like endless corridors of solitude, echoing with the whispers of her own fears.

But life doesn't stop moving, even when you wish it would. Zara soon found herself in yet another school and then another. Changing schools became a pattern, a way to escape the lingering memories and the harsh judgment of peers who couldn't feel her pain. It wasn't a quest for better education; it was a quest for sanctuary.

With each new school came a fresh set of challenges. The students were different, the routines unfamiliar, and the expectations varied. Zara had to adapt repeatedly like a chameleon, changing its colors to survive. It was a testament to her resilience and her ability to carry on despite the heavy baggage of her past.

But the journey was far from easy. In some schools, she encountered bullies who sensed her vulnerability. They pounced with cruel words and hurtful actions, further isolating her in a world that seemed determined to push her to the limit.

In others, the teachers were well-meaning but unaware of the storm within her. They couldn't fathom the depths of her trauma, and their efforts to help often fell short. Zara's silence became her shield, her way of protecting herself from prying eyes and sympathetic but empty gestures. No hand was reaching out to help her; she was all alone.

Through all these trials, she carried the weight of her secret, the heavy trauma of what had been taken from her. The assault had stolen not only her innocence but also her sense of belonging. She felt like an outsider, a puzzle piece that didn't fit into the picture.

Eventually, Zara's journey through schools led her to become a wanderer searching for a place to call home. It was a lonely path, one filled with uncertainty and isolation. The constant change had made it nearly impossible to form lasting friendships or find a sense of stability.

And so, she made a decision that would change the course of her educational journey once again. Zara chose to homeschool, to take control of her own destiny and carve a path that would allow her to heal and grow at her own pace. It was a brave choice, a declaration that she would no longer be defined by the darkness of her past.

But even in isolation, healing is possible. Zara's path was a testament to the resilience of the human spirit, a reminder that even in the darkest of times, there is a flicker of light waiting to be ignited. Her journey was far from over, but with each step, she was inching closer to a future where her past would no longer define her.

The trauma of Zara's assault cast a long shadow over her every school experience. Each new environment, with its unfamiliar faces and bustling hallways, felt like an assault on her senses. The voices, the hurried footsteps, the laughter of students—it all seemed too much, too overwhelming.

In her first school after the incident, Zara would often find herself shrinking into the shadows, trying to make herself invisible. She felt like everyone's gaze was a spotlight, exposing her vulnerabilities to the world. Every interaction, no matter how innocent, carried the weight of her past.

Her anxiety levels soared. The once-familiar routine of school became a daily battle, a battlefield where she fought to keep herself from falling. Panic attacks would strike without warning, leaving her breathless and trembling. The hallways that were supposed to lead to classrooms felt more like nightmares.

Changing schools was, in part, an attempt to escape the relentless triggers that each institution brought. But the relief was always temporary.

In one school, she encountered bullies who taunted her with cruel words, making her feel like an outcast in an already unfamiliar world. The pain of the assault was increased by the relentless cruelty of her peers, leaving her emotionally drained and traumatized.

In another school, well-intentioned teachers attempted to understand and help her. But the depth of her trauma was beyond their understanding. Their efforts often felt like empty gestures, like trying to mend broken pieces. Zara's silence became her armor, a way to protect herself from questions she couldn't bear to answer.

As she moved from one institution to another, it was as if she were constantly trapped in a whirlwind of new beginnings and painful endings. She yearned for stability, for a place where she could be herself without fear or judgment. But that distant relief seemed just out of reach.

The constant change took a toll on her ability to form connections. Friendships were fleeting. Zara longed for the warmth of lasting friendships, for the sense of belonging that had been stolen from her.

Through all these trials, she bore the weight of her secret. The assault had robbed her of her innocence, leaving her feeling broken.

She felt like an imposter, a stranger in her own life. The trauma echoed in her mind, a haunting space that drowned out the voices of those who tried to reach out to her.

But amidst the turmoil and chaos, Zara's spirit remained unbroken. She clung to the hope that someday she would find a place where she could heal, a space where she could rebuild what had been shattered.

The assault had left deep scars on Zara's soul, scars that extended far beyond the physical realm. One of the most profound impacts of the traumatic experience was her ability to trust in others. It was as if a bridge connecting her to the rest of the world had been burnt to ashes, leaving her emotionally isolated on an island of her own making.

Her ability to trust, something so natural and inherent to human connections, had been shattered that fateful day. The trust she once placed in people—the trust that should have been the foundation of friendships, relationships, and the bonds that hold society together—had crumbled. It had crumbled under the weight of betrayal and pain.

Zara had always been cautious about forming deep connections. Her struggles with social interactions, her encounters with bullies, and her experiences with the supernatural had already made her somewhat of an outsider in the world of friendships. But the assault had taken it to a whole new level.

Every smile became a mask, every word a potential weapon. She looked at the people around her through a different lens—a lens tainted by suspicion and fear. What if they, too, had hidden intentions? What if they, too, could hurt her in the most devastating way possible?

This mistrust was a heavy burden to bear. It weighed down her heart, creating a wall that separated her from the warmth of genuine human connections. She yearned for closeness, for the kind of trust that allows people to confide in each other, to lean on one another during difficult times. But the walls around her heart remained unbreakable.

The isolation was not just emotional; it was a cage she had built to protect herself from the possibility of ever experiencing such pain again. It was a shield that kept her safe but also increased her sense of loneliness. She had locked her emotions away, sealing them in a vault buried deep within her.

Even well-meaning attempts to reach out to her were met with resistance. The fear of being vulnerable, of opening herself up to potential hurt, was too great. Her emotional isolation had become a survival mechanism—a way to avoid further pain and betrayal.

This isolation affected her in more ways than she could count. It affected her ability to form meaningful relationships, to share her thoughts and feelings, and to seek the support she desperately needed. She carried the weight of her trauma alone, a burden that grew heavier with each passing day.

But Zara was not resigned to this fate. She knew that the assault had stolen many things from her, but she refused to let it steal her entire life. She yearned to break free from the chains of isolation, to trust again, to love again.

Zara's path had taken her through six different schools, each one a challenge, each one an opportunity for growth. The constant change, the new faces, the overwhelming environments—all were overstimulating for a girl who had already seen more than her fair share of the world's darkness. But even in these trying moments, Zara persevered.

Being sexually assaulted had shaken the very foundation of trust in her life. It had made her question the intentions of others and had led her down a path of emotional isolation. But Zara was not one to surrender to despair. She understood that healing was not a linear journey; it was a road with twists and turns, moments of darkness, and light.

As Zara's story unfolds, we see a young girl who, despite the weight of her experiences, still held the spark of resilience within her.

She faced the monsters of her past, not with blind optimism, but with a courage born of necessity. It was a courage that would carry her through the darkest tunnels of her journey.

Chapter 7: Homeschooling and Escaping the Pain

Life has a funny way of teaching us that sometimes, the path less traveled is the one we must take. Zara, who had already walked a road riddled with darkness, found herself standing at an uncertain time once again. But this time, she made a choice that would change her journey in ways she couldn't yet imagine.

Traditional schools, with their bustling hallways and crowded classrooms, had proven to be overwhelming for Zara. The trauma of the past still clung to her like a shadow, and the noise and chaos of these institutions were like thunderstorms in her mind. She longed for a safe place, a space where she could breathe freely without the weight of hostile environments bearing down on her.

So, she made a decision that would bring about significant change in her life. Zara chose homeschooling, a path less traveled by teenagers of her age. It wasn't an easy choice, but it was a choice she made for her own well-being, for a chance to escape the pain that had become unbearable.

The isolated journey of homeschooling was a bittersweet one. It offered peace from the harsh realities of traditional schooling, but it also meant a degree of isolation that weighed on her heart. Yet, Zara knew that this was a necessary step, a way to reclaim her voice and her sense of self.

As she delved into her studies at home, Zara began to unravel the complexities of her own mind. She discovered a love for learning that extended beyond textbooks, a curiosity that was no longer stifled by the judgment of others. It was a small victory, a glimmer of hope in the midst of her isolated journey.

Homeschooling was a world in itself, a place where Zara could finally find solace from the storms that had raged within her. The first days were tough; she had to adapt to a new routine, set her own schedule, and be her own teacher. But in the midst of these difficulties, there were advantages she hadn't expected.

One of the most significant benefits of homeschooling was the freedom it granted her. Zara could learn at her own pace, explore subjects that genuinely interested her and create an environment that nurtured her growth. No longer bound by the rigid structure of traditional schools, she felt like a bird released from its cage, free to spread her wings and soar.

Yet, homeschooling came with its own set of challenges. The isolation, the absence of classmates to share laughter with, the occasional doubts about whether she was learning enough—these were hurdles she had to overcome. But Zara was no stranger to bullying and mockery, and she faced these challenges head-on, determined to make the most of her newfound independence.

As Zara embarked on this uncharted path of homeschooling, she began to understand the true value of self-discovery. She immersed herself in her interests, spending hours immersed in books, art, and exploration. She had always felt like an outsider, but now she reveled in her uniqueness, cherishing the qualities that made her who she was.

Homeschooling allowed Zara to escape not only the strict environments of traditional schools but also the relentless pain that had haunted her for so long. It became a place of healing, a space where she could mend the wounds of the past and emerge stronger, and more resilient than ever.

Homeschooling provided Zara with a sense of security that she had rarely experienced before. Within the confines of her home, she could learn, grow, and heal at her own pace. The outside world, with its unpredictability and potential threats, seemed like a distant land best observed from the safety of her window.

The truth was, Zara had developed a deep mistrust of people. Her encounter with abuse had shattered her faith in the goodness of humanity. The scars, both physical and emotional, served as a constant reminder of the darkness that lurked in unexpected places. It was a heavy burden to carry, but she had no choice – it was her reality.

Meeting new people, especially in the unpredictable environment of traditional schools, had become a source of anxiety for her. She couldn't help but wonder about their intentions, whether they harbored hidden motives or concealed their true selves behind friendly masks. The prospect of forming friendships had lost its appeal; it seemed like a risk she was no longer willing to take.

In her cocoon of homeschooling, Zara could shield herself from the world's harshness. The walls around her were not just physical but emotional, providing a shield against potential harm. It was a lonely existence, but it was one she had chosen to protect herself, to heal her wounded spirit.

Zara found solace in the familiarity of her own space, where she was the master of her domain. Her books were her companions, her art her therapy, and her imagination her playground. She could explore the depths of her interests without fear of judgment or betrayal.

As she delved into her studies and passions, Zara realized that she didn't need the validation or acceptance of others to define her worth. She was enough, just as she was. The wounds of the past had left scars, but they were also a testament to her strength and resilience.

In the isolation of homeschooling, Zara learned to trust herself above all else. She was her own teacher, mentor, and friend. It was a form of self-reliance that would serve her well in the years to come. But little did she know that life had more lessons in store for her, ones that would challenge her newfound sense of security and force her to confront the world once again.

Zara's journey through homeschooling was more than just a way to escape the outside world; it was a quest for inner strength and healing. She knew that to move forward, she needed to distance herself from the traumatic events that had defined her past. It was a gradual process, one that demanded patience and self-compassion.

In the quiet hours of her homeschooling routine, Zara found a home within herself. She delved into books that transported her to different worlds, where heroes faced their own trials and emerged victorious. Their stories became a source of inspiration, reminding her that strength could be found even in the most unlikely of places.

Zara's art also played an important role in her healing journey. With each stroke of the brush, she poured her emotions onto the canvas. The vibrant colors and intricate details mirrored the complexity of her feelings. It was as if her art gave her a voice when words failed her, a way to express the pain, anger, and resilience that coexisted within her.

As the days turned into weeks and then months, Zara noticed a subtle shift within herself. The nightmares that had once plagued her began to lose their grip. The memories of the assault, while never truly fading, no longer had the power to paralyze her with fear. She was learning to compartmentalize her past, to tuck it away in the corners of her mind where it couldn't overshadow her present.

But healing was not a linear process. There were days when the weight of her experiences pressed down upon her, threatening to drag her back into the abyss of trauma. On those days, she allowed herself to feel the pain, to acknowledge the scars, and to reach out to the few people she had come to trust for support.

Zara's journey was marked by small victories and setbacks, but each step, whether forward or backward, was a testament to her resilience. She was slowly rebuilding her sense of self, piecing together the fragments of her shattered innocence. It was a puzzle with no clear picture, but she was determined to create something beautiful out of the chaos.

Her decision to distance herself from the traumatic events was an act of self-care, a way to protect her fragile sense of self. She had come to understand that healing was not about erasing the past but about finding the strength to carry it without being consumed by it.

And so, in the space of homeschooling, Zara's inner strength grew. She was like a wounded bird learning to fly again, testing her wings with caution but also with a newfound sense of freedom. Little did she know that this inner strength would soon be put to the test as life beckoned her back into the world beyond her safe haven.

As Zara gradually distanced herself from the traumatic events of her past, she was not erasing her history but rather learning to carry it without being overwhelmed by it. Her inner strength grew with each passing day, and she knew that one day, she would be ready to face the world once again.

Zara's experiences remind us that life's challenges do not define us; rather, it's how we respond to them that shapes our character. Her journey teaches us the importance of self-care, self-compassion, and the pursuit of inner strength. We are all survivors of our own stories, and Zara's story is a testament to the resilience that resides within each of us.

Chapter 8: The Silent Confidant

In the midst of darkness, a beacon of light often emerges unexpectedly. For Zara, her confidant in the storm of her life turned out to be someone she had never imagined – her host brother, Marson Anderson.

Marson, or Mar as he preferred to be called, was not the typical older brother figure. He was a few years older than Zara, with a quiet personality and a depth of understanding that seemed beyond his years. Perhaps it was the shared experience of being in the same household, or maybe it was an innate sense of connection that drew them together. Whatever the reason, their bond became a lifeline for Zara in the darkest of times.

In a world where Zara struggled to trust anyone, Mar was the only one she could truly rely on. He became the silent confidant she desperately needed. Their connection was unspoken, built on a foundation of shared glances, knowing smiles, and a mutual understanding of each other's pain.

Mar's presence was a source of peace for Zara. When the weight of her secrets and traumas threatened to overwhelm her, she would seek refuge in their shared moments. Late-night conversations in hushed tones, hidden away from the prying eyes and ears of their household, became their safe place.

They talked about everything – dreams, fears, hopes, and even the ghosts that Zara had seen since childhood. In Mar, she found someone who didn't judge her or label her as strange. Instead, he listened with an open heart and an open mind, offering comfort and validation.

One of the most beautiful aspects of their bond was the absence of judgment. Zara could reveal the depths of her pain, her fears, and the haunting memories of her past, knowing that Mar would not turn away. His silent support spoke volumes, a reminder that sometimes, words are not necessary to convey understanding and empathy.

In the midst of their lives, Zara and Mar forged a connection that was deeper than the boundaries of family. They became each other's pillars of strength, standing tall against the storms that raged around them.

As they navigated the challenges of their shared existence, Zara discovered the power of trust. She learned that vulnerability was not a weakness but a pathway to healing. Mar's supportive presence in her life allowed her to slowly release the shackles of her past and step into a future where she could reclaim her innocence.

Their silent confidantship was a source of hope and inspiration for Zara. It taught her that even in the darkest of circumstances, a single person could make a world of difference. It was a reminder that healing was possible, and that the journey toward recovery often began with a single, trusting heart.

Their connection wasn't limited to the confines of their home; they often adventured into the world together, seeking refuge in nature. The nearby woods became their sanctuary, a place where the rustling leaves and chirping birds provided a soothing backdrop to their conversations. There, they could shed the burdens of their past and simply be themselves.

Marson had a knack for turning these outings into small adventures. He would teach Zara about the various plants and animals they encountered, imparting his wisdom with an air of quiet authority. It was during these moments that Zara realized the depth of his knowledge and the gentleness of her host brother's spirit.

Their friendship also allowed Zara to experience the simple joys of life. Marson introduced her to the art of stargazing, and on clear nights, they would spread a blanket in the backyard and lose themselves in the vastness of the cosmos. Under the stars, Zara felt both small and deeply connected to the universe.

As the seasons changed, so did their adventures. They explored nearby meadows with wildflowers, took long walks along the riverbanks, and even tried their hand at gardening, nurturing tiny saplings into thriving plants. Each experience brought them closer, reinforcing the strength of their bond.

However, amidst the beauty of their friendship, there were moments of darkness that neither could escape. The memories of abuse still lingered, casting long shadows over their lives. Zara would sometimes wake up in the middle of the night, drenched in sweat, her heart pounding from nightmares of that traumatic night.

It was during one such night when Marson found her trembling in her room. Without a word, he sat beside her and held her until the fear went away. It was in those silent moments of comfort that Zara understood the true meaning of trust and unconditional support.

Their friendship was a lifeline, but it couldn't erase the scars of the past. Zara's trust in others remained fragile. Yet, she found solace in knowing that she didn't have to face her demons alone. Marson was there, a constant presence in her life, a silent confidant who offered support.

As days turned into weeks and weeks into months, the bond between Zara and Marson deepened. They had become each other's silent confidants, sharing the darkness of their pasts together, hand in hand.

One evening, as they sat on the porch, gazing at the setting sun painting the sky in hues of orange and pink, Zara couldn't help but marvel at how far they had come. The burdens they carried had drawn them closer, and their shared experiences had created an unspoken understanding between them.

It was during moments like these that Zara realized just how much Marson had been through in his own life. He had faced adversity with a quiet strength that she admired. While she had her own demons to battle, she knew that he carried his own share of scars.

One chilly winter's night, when the world outside was blanketed in snow, Marson finally opened up about his past. They were sitting by the fireplace, the flames casting dancing shadows on the walls.

"Zara," he began softly, his eyes fixed on the flickering flames, "I've never told anyone about this before."

She turned to him, her expression a mixture of curiosity and concern. "You don't have to if you're not ready," she replied gently.

But Marson had made up his mind to share his story. "I was orphaned at a young age," he began, his voice barely above a whisper. "My parents died in a car accident when I was just eight years old. I was left with no family, no one to turn to."

Zara listened intently, her heart aching for her friend. She had known that Marson had a difficult past, but hearing the details sent a shiver down her spine.

"I ended up in a foster home," he continued, his gaze distant as he relived those painful memories. "It wasn't an easy life. I moved from one home to another, always feeling like an outsider. There were times when I didn't know where my next meal would come from."

Tears welled up in Zara's eyes as she tried to imagine the young Marson, facing such hardships alone. She reached out and placed a comforting hand on his shoulder.

"But," he said, a faint smile touching his lips, "through it all, I never lost hope. I believed that someday, things would get better. And then, I met this family. They took me in, took care of me, and raised me. I cannot thank them enough."

Zara was deeply moved by Marson's resilience. She couldn’t imagine telling him what his father had truly been capable of and what he had done to her.

Their conversations often delved into the intricacies of life, philosophy, and the human experience. They shared their dreams and fears, their hopes and disappointments. Zara wanted to confide in Marson about the assault, her difficulty in trusting others, and her constant battle with self-doubt.

Their growing intimacy was not just about sharing their traumas; it was about embracing the present moment. They found solace in the simple act of being together, whether it was reading books side by side, taking long walks in the woods, or even sitting in companionable silence.

Days turned into weeks, and the heavy truth that Zara carried continued to weigh on her like an unbearable burden. Every moment spent with Marson was a reminder of the unspoken secret that threatened to shatter their bond.

It wasn't that Zara didn't want to tell him. She knew that Marson deserved to know the truth about his father's actions. Yet, the words remained trapped in the depths of her throat, as though held captive by an invisible force.

Each time she looked into Marson's eyes, she saw the innocence and trust that had grown between them. How could she be the one to shatter that trust? How could she reveal the darkness that lurked in the heart of someone he had loved and respected all his life?

The weight of her silence grew in her heart, squeezing tighter with each passing day. She longed for the relief that would come with sharing her painful secret, but the fear of the consequences held her back.

One evening, as they sat on the porch, the setting sun casting long shadows around them, Zara mustered the courage to broach the subject. But when she opened her mouth, the words refused to come out. She watched Marson, his features softened by the warm, golden light, and the truth felt like a dagger at the tip of her tongue.

"Is something on your mind, Zara?" Marson asked, his gaze filled with concern.

Zara swallowed hard, her throat dry. "It's just... I've been thinking a lot about your father lately."

Marson's expression darkened slightly, as though he sensed the weight of the unspoken words. "What about him?"

Zara hesitated, her heart pounding in her chest. She wanted to protect Marson, shield him from the pain that the truth would bring. But she also knew that he deserved to know.

"Marson," she began, her voice barely a whisper, "I wanted to ask you something."

He turned to her, his eyes searching her face. "What is it, Zara?"

She took a deep breath, her hands trembling. "It's about your father... do you love him?"

A heavy silence settled over them, the words hanging in the air. Zara watched as Marson's expression shifted from calm to confusion. “I do,” he answered, his voice soft yet trembling with fear.

At that moment, Zara realized that the truth had the power to wound as deeply as any lie. She had the power to open a door to a painful reality, one that would forever change their lives and the nature of their relationship.

Chapter 9: The Weight of Disclosure

During a difficult conversation on the porch, Zara had realized that she could not reveal the truth to her host brother. She had started this conversation with the hope that she could share her pain with her brother, but seeing that he loved and idolized his father, she couldn't speak her truth.

Silence fell as Zara found herself speechless. But as Marson's eyes avoided hers, as his voice quivered with love for a father who had caused her so much pain, Zara couldn't bring herself to shatter his world. She couldn't be the one to turn his love into ashes, to force him to confront the terrible truth.

Instead, she withdrew the words that had been on the tip of her tongue, the words that would have torn their world apart. "Never mind," she whispered, her voice breaking as she forced a smile. "It's not important."

Marson turned back to the window, his gaze distant as he lost himself in thought. Zara knew she had made a choice, one that would keep Marson in the comforting embrace of his illusions. But in doing so, she had also chosen to carry the burden of her secret a little while longer. The weight of it pressed down on her, threatening to suffocate her, but she stayed silent.

As the night stretched on, neither of them spoke of what had almost been revealed. Instead, they went into their own thoughts, each burdened by their own secrets, their own pain. In the darkness of their shared silence, they found a sense of peace.

And so, the night wore on, and Zara clung to the fragile hope that maybe, just maybe, there was a way to heal without causing more pain, a way to protect the ones she loved from the harsh realities she had endured. It was a heavy burden to bear, but in the silence of that night, it was a burden she chose to carry.

Zara carried a secret so heavy that it seemed to have its own gravitational pull, constantly pulling her thoughts back to it. She had to make a decision, one that felt like walking on a tightrope. Should she tell Marson, her host brother, about what had happened between her and his father?

Ever since that evening on the porch, when their conversation had taken an unexpected turn, the atmosphere between them had changed. Marson had grown distant, his eyes clouded with questions he couldn't voice. Zara could sense the unspoken tension, and it was becoming very evident to Marson that she may be hiding something.

The promise Zara had made to herself, to Marson, to find the courage to share the truth, weighed heavily on her. She didn't want to see Marson struggle, his normally bright eyes to become filled with confusion. And she couldn't bear the crushing weight of this secret any longer.

Night after night, Zara tossed and turned in her bed, staring up at the ceiling. The dim light of her bedside lamp cast dark shadows on her diary, waiting for the words that had been trapped within her for so long to be set free.

With trembling hands and tears in her eyes, she began to write, each word unlocking a painful memory into the pages of her diary.

"Marson," she wrote, "I don't know how to say this, but I can't keep it hidden any longer. Your father... he did something terrible to me, something I can't forget or forgive."

As Zara continued to write, she poured out her heart, remembering the horrifying details of that night. She described the paralyzing fear that had gripped her, the pain that still echoed through her body and soul. She wanted Marson to understand the torment of carrying such a heavy secret, of watching him change without knowing the cause.

Zara confessed the agony of living a lie, how it had eaten away at her, emptying her out from the inside. She knew that sharing the truth would be painful, that it might shatter Marson's world, but she also knew that living with this hidden truth was a torment that needed to end.

As she closed her diary, Zara felt a strange mixture of relief and anxiety. The weight of her secret was no longer hers alone to bear. She had exposed her vulnerability, laid bare her pain, and now she had to wait. The future was uncertain, and Zara could only hope that Marson would find the strength to face the truth and that their bond would prove resilient enough to endure whatever storm lay ahead.

As time passed, Zara's secret grew heavier, like a dark cloud that never left her side. The truth about Marson's father's assault weighed on her heart, and the fear of what might happen if it ever came out consumed her.

Zara and Marson had become close, sharing their deepest thoughts and fears. Their bond was a lifeline in their tough world. But Zara was afraid that revealing the truth might shatter that bond. She worried about how Marson would react—would he blame her? Would he hate her for keeping such a huge secret?

Her fear wasn't just about their relationship. Zara also struggled with a moral dilemma. By staying silent, was she protecting someone who didn't deserve it? Was she allowing harm to continue? It was a heavy burden to bear.

The nights were the hardest. Alone in the dark, Zara couldn't escape the memories of the assault. She felt guilty for not speaking up, for not stopping it from happening again. Zara's mind was a battlefield of emotions. She feared losing Marson's trust, but she also knew that keeping the truth hidden might be wrong.

But in the midst of her fears, there was a small hope. Zara believed that one day, she'd find the strength to reveal the truth, not to hurt Marson but to protect others. She hoped their bond could survive the storm of disclosure and come out even stronger.

As Zara struggled with these unspoken fears, she held onto that hope, a promise to herself that, one day, she'd find the courage to speak her truth and break free from the weight of her silence.

Zara couldn't escape the fact that the truth was like a ticking time bomb. Every day she held onto it, the more dangerous it became. But revealing it was no simple task. As she pondered her options, her mind played out various scenarios, each with its own set of consequences.

She imagined telling Marson everything without holding back and sharing her deepest pain with the only person she could confide in. In this scenario, Zara would sit down with Marson and reveal the painful truth about his father. She imagined his reaction—a mixture of shock, anger, and sadness. He might feel betrayed that she hadn't told him earlier. But would their bond survive? Zara hoped that their friendship was strong enough to weather this storm, and that Marson would appreciate her honesty.

The second option was to continue bearing the weight of the secret on her own. Zara thought about how she could endure it, how she could protect Marson from the truth. She knew it might eat her up inside, but she was willing to sacrifice her peace of mind for the sake of their relationship. But would Marson eventually find out anyway, and what would that do to their trust?

Zara also thought about reaching out to adults she could trust, like her own parents or a counselor, and revealing the truth to them. They might have a better understanding of how to handle the situation and ensure Marson's safety. But this scenario raised its own set of questions. What if they didn't believe her, or worse, if they blamed her for not speaking up sooner?

Zara considered confronting Marson's father herself for his abusive behavior. But she knew it was a dangerous path, one that could put her in direct harm's way. She didn't want to worsen the situation, potentially risking Marson's safety.

As she weighed these scenarios, Zara's heart raced. The emotional wounds were deep, and each choice was filled with uncertainty. She didn't know which path to take, but one thing was clear—she couldn't carry this burden forever. The truth had to come out, and she had to find the courage to face the consequences, whatever they may be.

In the quiet of her room, Zara knew that this decision weighed not only on her shoulders but also on her fragile relationship with Marson. As she gazed out of her window, she wondered about the paths she could take, each shadowed by fear. The truth was a heavy burden, but so was the weight of silence.

Zara's journey through abuse and deception had taught her that sometimes, the most challenging choices were the ones that demanded the most courage. She knew that whatever she decided, it would have a profound impact on her life, on Marson's life, and on the fragile bond they had built. In the end, she realized that there was no easy way out, no painless path to take.

As she lay on her bed, the moonlight casting a gentle glow on her face, Zara made a silent promise to herself. She would find the strength to make the choice to reveal the truth someday, even if it meant facing the storm that the truth would unleash. She knew that her journey was far from over and that the path ahead was uncertain, but she was determined to face it head-on, armed with the belief that the truth, no matter how painful, had the power to heal and bring about change.

Zara's journey had transformed her innocence. She learned that innocence wasn't about ignorance; it was about keeping a pure heart and believing in the power of goodness, even in the face of darkness.

As she faced the challenging decision of whether to reveal the painful truth to her host brother, Zara stood strong. Her journey had taken her through the darkest of times, but it had also revealed an unshakable resilience within her. She was no longer the innocent child she once was; she had grown into a strong girl with an unbreakable human spirit.

This path from innocence to wisdom, from vulnerability to strength, had shaped Zara into an extraordinary individual. It was a journey that had molded her into who she was, and it was one that would continue to guide her to create her own identity.

Chapter 10: Shattered Bonds

The day had finally arrived, a day Zara had been dreading for a long time. She had carried the weight of the truth like a heavy stone, and today was the day she decided it couldn't burden her any longer. She needed to share it with Marson, her host brother, the one person she had grown to trust and confide in.

As she sat in her room, the walls seemed to close in on her. Her heart raced, and her palms were sweaty. She had rehearsed the words she wanted to say a hundred times, but now, when the moment had come, her voice felt stuck in her throat.

Marson knocked on her door, a concerned look in his eyes. "Zara, are you okay? You've been in here for a while."

Zara took a deep breath, her hands trembling. She knew there was no turning back. She needed to shatter the bonds of deception that had kept them apart. "Marson," she began, her voice shaky, "there's something I need to tell you."

He sat down beside her, his eyes locked onto hers. "What is it, Zara?"

The truth spilled out, painful and raw. Zara told him about the assault, about his own father's betrayal. She watched as his face contorted in disbelief, anger, and sadness. The room seemed to grow heavy with the weight of their shared pain.

Marson's voice quivered as he asked, "Why didn't you tell me sooner?"

Zara felt tears welling up in her eyes. "I was afraid, Marson. I didn't want to hurt you. I thought you loved your father, and I didn't want to shatter your world."

As the truth hung in the air like a heavy storm cloud, Marson's emotions were all over the place. He stood up abruptly, his chair scraping against the floor. "You're telling me that my father... did this to you..." His voice trailed off, unable to articulate the horror and disbelief that burned within him.

Zara nodded, tears streaming down her face. "I'm so sorry, Marson. I didn't know how to tell you."

He turned away from her, his fists clenched at his sides. "How could you keep something like this from me? When did this happen?"

Zara's voice quivered as she replied, "It happened a while ago, but I was scared to tell you sooner. Scared of what it would do to you, to us."

Marson's shoulders heaved with anger and sorrow. He felt betrayed not only by his father but also by the person he had come to trust the most. "You should have told me, Zara. I deserved to know the truth."

Tears welled up in Zara's eyes as she reached out to him. "I know, Marson, and I'm so sorry. I should have told you sooner, but I didn't want to hurt you."

He turned to face her, his eyes filled with a mixture of pain and anger. "You think keeping it from me would hurt less? You think protecting me from the truth was the right thing to do?"

Zara's heart ached as she realized the depth of her mistake. She had thought she was shielding him from pain, but she had only prolonged the inevitable. "I was wrong, Marson. I see that now. I should have told you, no matter how difficult it might have been."

Marson's anger began to fade away, replaced by a profound sadness as he watched Zara's tears flow freely. He stepped closer to her, his voice softer but still tinged with sorrow. "I'm not hurt, Zara. I just cannot believe you have been hurting for so long and you didn't tell me. You were suffering all alone, living in the corners of this darkness without saying a word. Do you know how much courage it takes? To bear an open wound without uttering a word?" His voice quivered as he spoke. "I'm sad that you thought you couldn't tell me, and you fought this internal battle."

Zara looked into Marson's eyes, her own filled with regret and longing for the bond they had shared. "No, Marson. This is not on you," she replied, her head shaking. "I thought I was protecting you, but I see now that I was wrong. I was so afraid of causing you pain that I kept my own suffering hidden. It was a mistake, and I'm sorry."

Marson reached out and gently wiped away her tears. "We both made mistakes, Zara. I should have noticed your pain earlier. I should have been there for you."

They stood there in the dimly lit room, two souls battered by their past, trying to find a way to heal together. The weight of the truth hung heavy between them, but so did the realization that they still cared for each other deeply.

Zara whispered, "What do we do now, Marson?"

He looked at her with determination in his eyes. "We heal, together. We face this darkness together, just like we've faced everything else."

Marson, his voice shaky but resolute, spoke gently, "Zara, we need to talk about what happened. I want to understand everything, to help you heal."

Zara nodded, her eyes brimming with tears. She took a deep breath and began recounting the horrifying incident, the words quivering as they left her lips. "It was a night that I can never forget, Marson. I had gone to bed early, as usual. The house was quiet, and I thought everyone was asleep. But then he came into my room..."

Marson's grip on her hand tightened as he listened, his own eyes welling up. He struggled to find words, his voice choked with emotion. "I'm so sorry, Zara. I can't imagine what you went through."

Tears streamed down Zara's face as she continued, the memories too painful to contain any longer. "I tried to scream, to fight back, but he was so much stronger. I felt so powerless, so violated. And the worst part is that I blamed myself for it, as if I had done something wrong."

Marson's tears fell freely now as he held her close, their shared pain creating an unbreakable bond between them. "Zara, none of this is your fault. You didn't deserve any of it."

Zara buried her face in Marson's shoulder, her body trembling with sobs. "I know that now, but it took me so long to accept it. I was so scared to tell anyone, especially you. I thought you would hate me."

Marson gently lifted her chin, their eyes meeting. "Zara, I could never hate you. I love you, and I'm here for you, no matter what. We'll get through this together."

As Zara's tears subsided, Marson held her close, his anger simmering just below the surface. He couldn't help but feel an overwhelming surge of rage toward his own father, a man he had once idolized.

"Zara," he began, his voice trembling with a mixture of anger and shame, "I can't believe my own father could do something so despicable. I looked up to him, and respected him. And now... I can't even look him in the eye."

Zara nodded, understanding the anger within Marson. "I know it's hard, Marson. But remember, this isn't your fault. You didn't know. None of us did."

Marson clenched his fists, his jaw set. "That doesn't change the fact that I should have protected you, Zara. I should have been there for you, and I wasn't."

Zara gently cupped his face, her eyes filled with compassion. "Marson, you are dealing with your own struggles. It's not your responsibility to protect me from everything."

Marson's anger began to shift, replaced by a profound sense of guilt. "I still wish I had done something, anything, to stop him. I can't believe I was living under the same roof as a monster."

Zara sighed, her heart aching for Marson. "We were both trapped, Marson, in different ways. But now, we have each other. And together, we can heal."

Marson leaned his forehead against Zara's, their breaths mingling as they shared a moment of deep connection. "I promise you, Zara, I'll make sure he pays for what he did."

Their relationship, once a sanctuary of trust and understanding, now felt fragile and strained. The emotional fallout from the revelation was tearing them apart, and Zara didn't know if they could ever rebuild what had been shattered.

After finally finding the courage to reveal the painful truth to Marson, a sense of relief washed over Zara. It was as if she had unburdened her soul, freeing herself from the heavy shackles of silence that had bound her for so long. The weight that had pressed upon her chest, suffocating her, had been lifted, and in its place, there was a newfound sense of lightness.

Sharing her secret with Marson had been both terrifying and liberating. She had feared his reaction, worried that he might blame himself or turn away from her in disgust. But instead, his response had been one of compassion and understanding, leaving her with a sense of gratitude.

Zara had spent countless nights replaying the scenario in her mind, questioning whether she should reveal the truth. She had wrestled with her inner demons, wondering if she could bear to revisit the trauma by uttering the words aloud. And now, with the truth laid bare, she felt like a weight had been lifted off her shoulders.

Yet, this newfound freedom was not without its challenges. She felt vulnerable and exposed, as if she had bared her soul to the world. There were moments when she questioned whether she had made the right choice, whether the truth had been worth the emotional turmoil it had unleashed.

But as time passed, Zara came to realize that the act of sharing had been a crucial step in her healing process. It had allowed her to confront the demons of her past, to acknowledge the pain she had endured, and to seek the support she needed to move forward. It was a testament to her strength and resilience, a reminder that even in the face of unspeakable darkness, she had the power to reclaim her voice.

The disclosure had not only deepened her bond with Marson but had also opened the door to a future where she could begin to rebuild her life. It was a chapter in her journey through abuse and deception that marked a turning point, a moment of renewal.

The revelation hung heavily in the air, like an unspoken truth that refused to fade away. Zara and Marson sat in the dimly lit room, both lost in their thoughts, both forever changed by the words that had been spoken.

For Marson, the news had shattered him in every way. On one hand, he was furious at his father for the unspeakable act he had committed, and on the other, he was consumed by guilt for not having protected Zara. He couldn't help but question his own innocence in the matter, wondering if he could have done something more to shield her from harm.

Meanwhile, Zara grappled with her own set of emotions. While the disclosure had brought relief in some ways, it had also made her revisit the painful memories that she had buried deep within herself. Nightmares haunted her sleep, and flashbacks haunted her waking hours.

Their relationship, too, underwent a transformation. The deep bond they had always shared grew even stronger as they became each other's pillars of support. Marson's commitment to her healing process was a source of comfort for Zara, a reminder that she was not alone in her journey.

But it wasn't all smooth sailing. There were moments of anger and frustration, times when they couldn't bear the weight of their shared pain. Yet, they persevered, knowing that they were each other's best chance at healing and finding closure.

Chapter 11: Rebuilding from Ruins

The truth had been laid bare, a heavy burden lifted, and a bond strengthened. Zara and Marson had confronted the darkest chapter of their shared journey, but this was not the end—it was the beginning of a new phase, one where they could rebuild from the ruins of their past.

The revelation of the sexual assault had changed their lives forever. For Marson, it meant a very big shift in his relationship with his father. The man he had once idolized was now seen in a different light, tainted by the truth. Marson struggled with a storm of conflicting emotions—anger, betrayal, and a deep sense of shame that he had not been there to protect Zara.

Conversations with Zara had become both a source of solace and anguish for Marson. He felt an overwhelming desire to support her in any way he could, to be the pillar she could lean on, but he also felt the weight of his own emotional turmoil.

Slowly but surely, the nightmares that had haunted her for so long began to lose their grip. Those sleepless nights gave way to peaceful slumber. Panic attacks, once an unstoppable force, became less frequent. Zara was learning to tame the demons that had held her captive.

Marson stood by her side, his support showing how unbreakable their bond truly was. Their relationship had transformed into something deeper and more profound. He had his own battles to fight, and demons to confront, but they faced them together. Their shared experiences created an unspoken understanding, a silent pact of resilience.

Her parents, once oblivious to her struggles, underwent their own transformation. They listened, learned, and, most importantly, believed in their daughter's strength. They couldn't change the past, but they could be a beacon of support as she forged ahead.

In the ruins of their past, Zara found the bricks to build a future. It was a future marked by resilience, empathy, and a fierce determination to ensure that the horrors they had endured would not define them. This was her story—a story of survival, of rebuilding, and of finding light in the darkest of places.

Zara knew that the road ahead would still be challenging, but she was armed with newfound strength and an unshakeable belief in her ability to thrive. She had emerged from the ruins stronger than ever before, a testament to the human spirit's remarkable capacity to heal and grow.

After the climactic revelation, Zara had embarked on her own profound journey. It was a journey towards healing, self-acceptance, and the quest to find her own path in the world. The impact of her struggles had left deep scars, but she was determined to transform them into symbols of her true strength and power.

The path to healing was not a straight line; it was filled with ups and downs, moments of self-doubt, and times when the past threatened to pull her back into its dark echoes. But with Marson, her friends, and her newfound strength, she learned to move forward step by step, closer to a new beginning.

Zara started by accepting herself, flaws and all. She realized that her past didn't define her; it was simply a chapter in her story. She began to see her uniqueness as a source of strength, not weakness. Her struggles had sculpted her into a person of depth and uniqueness in a world full of ordinary minds.

Zara's resilience was her greatest asset. She faced her fears with great courage, refusing to let them dictate her life. Slowly but surely, she began to rebuild the trust that had been shattered, not just in others but in herself as well.

Finding her own path was a liberating experience. Zara explored her passions, discovered new interests, and realized that life held endless possibilities. She pursued her artistic talents with strength, using painting as a way to express the emotions she could never put into words.

Through it all, she held onto hope. Hope that the future would be brighter than the past. Hope that her story would inspire others to find their strength and heal. Hope that, in her journey through abuse and deception, she could show how to not be consumed by the darkness.

She emerged from the ruins not as a victim, but as a survivor, stronger and wiser than she had ever imagined. Her journey was far from over, but she faced the future with a newfound sense of purpose and a heart filled with resilience.

Healing wasn't always easy. As Zara walked the path of healing, there were moments when the pain of her past came rushing back like a tidal wave. It was as if the memories were locked in a box, waiting for the right moment to break free.

Some days, a simple sight or sound would trigger a vivid recollection of the trauma she had endured. The assault, the isolation, the fear - it all came rushing back, threatening her sense of safety once again. These moments were like reopening old wounds, and the pain was raw and intense.

But Zara had learned to face these memories head-on. She didn't shy away from the pain; instead, she embraced it as a part of her journey. She allowed herself to cry, to scream, to feel the anger and the sorrow that had been buried deep inside her for so long. Because it isn't through hiding our pain that we display deep courage, but it is when we let the pain touch our souls and let it leave that we can truly be brave.

It was through these moments of remembrance that she found her strength. Each time she confronted the ghosts of her past, she emerged a little stronger, a little more resilient. She refused to let the pain define her; instead, she used it as a source of motivation to keep moving forward.

Zara knew that healing wasn't about erasing the past; it was about making peace with it. She couldn't change what had happened to her, but she could change how it shaped her future. And so, she carried the weight of her memories with grace, knowing that they were a part of her, but not the entirety of her being.

In the darkest of moments, Zara found the light of her own resilience. She knew that her journey was an ode to the power of the human spirit to overcome even the most traumatic of experiences. And as she looked back at the ruins of her past, she saw not just pain, but the foundation upon which she was building a brighter, stronger future.

As Zara stood at this point in her life, she couldn't help but reflect on the journey that had brought her here. It was a journey that had started with the loss of innocence, a journey through abuse and deception that had shaken her to her core. But it was also a journey of resilience, strength, and self-discovery.

She thought back to the early years of her life when she had been born into privilege, yet isolated by her struggles. The attempted assault, the haunting visions, the difficulty in making friends - all of these experiences had left scars on her soul. She had been a girl trapped in a world of secrets, a world where her voice had been silenced.

Then came the time in her life where she was sent to live with a host family in a rural area, seeking a fresh start. It had been a mixed bag of experiences, with moments of joy and challenges. The assault had been a dark cloud in that chapter, a traumatic event that had threatened to consume her.

The revelation had shattered the fragile bonds of her relationship with her host brother, Marson, yet it had also brought them closer in unexpected ways. They had embraced the storm together, supporting each other through the emotional breakdowns. It had been a painful process, but one that had ultimately set them both free from the weight of their secrets.

Zara had chosen the path of healing, of self-acceptance, and finding her own way. She had learned that therapy wasn't the only route to healing; sometimes, the greatest therapy came from within. She had embraced her pain, her memories, and used them as stepping stones towards a brighter future.

Now, as she stood at the threshold of a new beginning, Zara knew that her journey was far from over. Life was a continuous series of chapters, each one offering the opportunity for growth and transformation. She had discovered her inner strength, her resilience, and her ability to rebuild from the ruins of her past.

With a sense of purpose and a newfound understanding of herself, Zara was ready to face the world with renewed courage. She had lost her innocence along the way, but in its place, she had found something even more precious - her authentic self. The journey through abuse and deception had shaped her, but it had not defined her. She was a survivor, a warrior, and she was determined to live life on her own terms.

As she looked ahead, the horizon seemed vast and full of possibilities. Zara took a deep breath, ready to step into the next chapter of her life with courage, resilience, and a heart filled with hope. The girl who had once been lost was now found, and she was ready to write her own story.

In the end, Zara's journey through abuse and deception was not just a story of pain and suffering. It was a story of resilience, growth, and the unbreakable human spirit. It was a journey that had tested her in ways she could never have imagined, but it had also revealed her inner strength and capacity for healing.

As she looked toward the future, Zara knew that her past would always be a part of her, but it would not define her. She had learned that scars were not signs of weakness; they were badges of survival. Every challenge she had faced, every obstacle she had overcome, had shaped her into the person she was becoming.

Zara had found peace in her own company, strength in vulnerability, and courage in the face of her darkest fears. She had discovered the power of truth, the healing powers of self-acceptance, and the beauty of authentic connections. Her bond with Marson, her host brother, was a testament to the resilience of the human heart.

The future held the promise of new beginnings, fresh adventures, and the opportunity to live life on her own terms. Zara was determined to make the most of it, to embrace each day with gratitude and hope. She knew that the path ahead might not always be smooth, but she was ready to face it with her frown turned upside down.

In her journey, she had found her voice, and she was determined to use it to speak her truth and advocate for those who couldn't. Zara had transformed from a girl who had lost her innocence to a woman who had found her strength.

As she stepped into the unknown, she carried with her the lessons of her past, the resilience of her spirit, and the strong belief that no matter how dark the night, there would always be a dawn. Zara's story was a testament to the human capacity for healing, growth, and the rediscovery of lost innocence. And as she walked into the future, she knew that the best chapters of her life were yet to be written.

Chapter 12: Healing and Redemption

In the quiet spaces of her heart, Zara found the strength to heal. It was a journey through shadows, but within those shadows, she discovered a light that refused to fade out. Each step forward was a victory, an example of the resilience that lay at the core of her being.

The scars of the past were no longer chains; they were badges of honor. They told a story of survival, of a girl who refused to be defined by the darkness that had once threatened to consume her.

She learned to be her own hero, to wrap herself in self-love and self-acceptance. It wasn't about erasing the past; it was about rewriting her story. Zara's heart, once fragile, now beat with a quiet strength that resonated through her every step.

Through the trials and tribulations, Zara had found her voice. It echoed through her soul, a melody of truth. She spoke not just for herself, but for all those whose voices had been silenced by the weight of their own stories. Zara became a sign of hope, a living testament to the power of transformation.

Her journey was a testament to the human spirit's capacity for resilience. Zara was not just surviving; she was thriving. The same girl who had once seen ghosts now saw her own reflection in the mirror - a warrior, a survivor, a force to be reckoned with.

The love and support she found along the way were the stitches that held her wounded soul together. Her bond with Marson, her host brother, remained a source of her strength.

As Zara stood at the point of a new beginning, she looked back at the girl she once was. She was no longer defined by her struggles; she was defined by her triumphs. Zara had discovered that true healing wasn't about erasing the scars; it was about wearing them with pride.

Her story was one of redemption, of a lost innocence that had been found again in the depths of her own soul. Zara's journey through abuse and deception had led her to a place of strength, compassion, and unshakeable belief in oneself.

And as she stepped into the embrace of her future, Zara knew that she carried within her a light that could never be dimmed. In every page of her story, Zara's journey was a lesson of hope for all those who had ever felt lost, for in the heart of adversity, Zara had found her way back to herself.

Zara continued to walk her path with a newfound purpose, knowing that her journey was not just for herself, but for all those who needed to hear that they were not alone.

She became an advocate, a voice for the voiceless and the victims of abuse. Through her words, she offered solace and strength to others who had known the sting of betrayal and the weight of silence. Zara's story resonated far beyond the pages of her own life, touching hearts and igniting sparks of hope in even the darkest corners of the world.

Her relationship with Marson deepened a bond that transcended the scars of their pasts. They became the proof that even in the face of unimaginable pain, the human spirit could rise, stronger and more beautiful than ever before.

As the years passed, Zara's light only grew brighter. Her presence was a reminder that no matter how broken, or scarred, there was always a path forward.

Her story became a torch for those still finding their way through the darkness. She stood as living proof that even the deepest wounds could transform into sources of light and strength.

As she looked back on her journey, Zara knew that while the scars would always be a part of her, they were no longer her defining feature. She was a survivor, a warrior, a testament to the indomitable human spirit.

And so, the final chapter of her book was not an ending, but a beginning. It was a call to all those who felt lost and broken, a promise that there was a path forward, no matter how obscured it may seem.

For in the end, Zara's story was not just one of loss and pain. It was a story of redemption, of the extraordinary power that lies within each of us to heal, to grow, and to reclaim our lost innocence.

In the quiet echoes of Zara's journey, there echoed a powerful message - one that resonated far beyond the pages of her own life. It was a message of hope, resilience, and the unyielding strength that lies within every human heart.

Zara's story was a hope for those who felt trapped in the shadows of their own pain. It was a reminder that they were not alone, that their voices mattered, and that healing was possible. Through the storms of her life, she had emerged with extraordinary power that resides within us all.

Zara knew that silence could be as imprisoning as any physical chains. She encouraged others to find their voices, to break free from the shackles of secrecy, and to seek the support and love they deserved.

Above all, Zara's journey reflected the strength of the human spirit. It showed that even in the darkest moments, there was a glimmer of light, a spark of hope that could ignite a transformation. Her resilience was a reminder that no matter the depths of despair, we each held the power to rise. It whispered that no matter the trials we face, we are never truly alone. That within each of us lies a strength waiting to be discovered.

And so, as the final words of her story settled into the hearts of those who read them, they carried with them a profound truth - that the journey from lost innocence to reclaimed strength was not just possible, but within the reach of us all.

Her ability to transform herself after years of abuse, is a reminder that even in the darkest moments, there is a glimmer of light waiting to pierce through.

Her journey from the depths of despair to the heights of resilience echoed a universal truth: that within every soul lies an untapped source of power. It called out to those who had known pain, who had felt the weight of silence, urging them to take that first step towards healing.

Her story shows that wounds could transform into scars, and scars into badges of strength and that adversity was not the end of the story, but the beginning of a new, empowered chapter.

As her story echoed in the hearts of those who needed it, it displays a rallying cry for change. It called on society to listen, to believe, and to stand with survivors. It demanded a world where no one needed to suffer in silence, where the strength of the collective could shatter the chains of abuse.

And so, as Zara's journey found its place in the annals of countless lives, it left behind a legacy of hope, resilience, and the belief that no matter the trials we face, we have the power to rise. It whispered to the wounded hearts of the world: "You are not alone. Your strength is boundless. You are capable of reclaiming your light."

In the end, Zara's story was not just about her. It was about the indomitable spirit that courses through us all, waiting for the moment when we choose to let it shine. It was about the potential within each of us to heal, to grow, and to reclaim the lost pieces of our innocence.

Zara's journey is about the young girl who began her life in a world of privilege, yet was marked by struggles beyond her years. Her innocence, though lost in the darkest tides of life, was never truly gone. It was simply transformed, melted into her strength.

From the early days of seeing ghostly encounters and finding solace in imaginary friends, to the painful attempts at connection and the assault that shook her foundation, each chapter of Zara's story held a thread of resilience. She carried these experiences, not as burdens, but as pieces of her broken self.

Sent to a rural host family, she discovered a side of herself she never knew existed. The open fields and quiet nights held a mirror to her inner strength. It was a time of reckoning, of understanding that being unique was not a flaw, but a source of power.

The shadows of abuse, though traumatic, did not break Zara. They built in her a determination to rise above, to find her voice amidst the pain. The assault was a chapter, not the whole story. This is a reminder that appearances can be deceiving, and that behind closed doors, even the seemingly perfect have their battles.

Her journey through schools, filled with overstimulation and overwhelming encounters, led her to the sanctuary of homeschooling. In her own space, she found her own peace inside herself. The weight of revelation hung heavy, but Zara's courage in sharing her truth was a lesson for all who carry their pain in silence.

Marson, her silent confidant, showed her that despite the darkness, there are still good people around and that they are worth looking for and confiding in. Their connection was a lifeline, a reminder that in the darkest moments, there can be light. The revelation of his father's assault was a turning point, a difficult truth that tested the strength of their bond.

The aftermath brought both pain and healing. Zara's decision to disclose, though fraught with fear, was a step towards her own redemption. The scars of her past, once open wounds, were now marks of resilience. She chose not therapy, but the path of self-discovery, a journey that led her to rebuild from the ruins.

And now, as I stand with Zara at the threshold of her future, I see not just a survivor, but a beacon of hope. Her story is a testament to the human spirit, to the capacity for healing, and to the power of speaking out against abuse.

As Zara steps into the light, she carries with her the collective strength of all who have faced adversity and emerged stronger. Her journey speaks to the resilience that resides within us all, waiting for the moment when we choose to let it shine.

In Zara's story, we find not just a tale of loss, but a narrative of hope. It is a reminder that our innocence, no matter how shattered, is never truly lost. It is within us, waiting for us to rediscover it, waiting for us to reclaim our light.

Printed in Great Britain
by Amazon

0966b979-305f-4f45-885c-ad3f5a78b4d1R01